Blessed Journey, FELLOW TRAVELER

Rosalie Gilliland

WESTBOW
PRESS®
A DIVISION OF THOMAS NELSON
& ZONDERVAN

WestBow Press books may be ordered through booksellers or by contacting:

WestBow Press
A Division of Thomas Nelson & Zondervan
1663 Liberty Drive
Bloomington, IN 47403
www.westbowpress.com
844-714-3454

New King James Version (NKJV)
Scripture taken from the New King James Version®. Copyright © 1982 by Thomas Nelson. Used by permission. All rights reserved.

ISBN: 979-8-3850-2595-4 (sc)
ISBN: 979-8-3850-2596-1 (e)

Library of Congress Control Number: 2024910490

Print information available on the last page.

WestBow Press rev. date: 06/13/2024

DEDICATION

I wish to dedicate this book to my sons, Max, Justin, Steven and Matthew, my daughter(in-law) Laura, and my precious granddaughter Abigail. Thank you for always keeping me accountable, and for not holding my mistakes against me. Because of all of you, I consider myself the most blessed of women.

Chapter 1
IN THE BEGINNING

FOR MANY BELIEVERS, THE ROAD TO SALVATION CAN BE A BUMPY, CONFUSING, emotional journey. The life he/she is leaving behind pulls heavily, as does the world. To the unbelieving, the life of a Born Again Christian appears boring at best; at worst, detached from reality. The unsaved are simply unable to comprehend how much God fills the life of a believer, and is his/her anchor. Nowhere in the world can the true peace of God be found outside of a relationship with Him; that gift alone is worth the whole world. But there is so much more.

Most people don't understand the distinction between religion and Christianity, as Christianity is not a religion. Christianity began when Jesus, the "Christ," initiated His followers into a belief system of faith in Him as one entity of the triune God. Unique among belief systems is Christianity's worship of the Holy Trinity, which should not be confused with polytheism - the numerous, fabricated, impersonal gods of other religions. Islam's Quran stating "There is no deity but God alone; He has no partner with him..." is intended as a reproach to Christianity.

Throughout history, mankind has established numerous theologies, a few even based on Scripture to some degree. But every man-made religion misses the mark, in that accepting the work Jesus performed on the cross alone is the only path to salvation. Leading an upstanding life, donating generously to the poor, reciting the same prayerful passage

1

repeatedly will not secure anyone's salvation. "And when you pray, do not use vain repetitions as the heathen do. For they think that they will be heard for their many words." (Matthew 6:7)

As previously mentioned, Christianity is unique among the world's faiths for its fundamental belief of salvation through Christ alone. "Nor is there salvation in any other, for there is no other name under Heaven given among men by which we must be saved." (Acts 4:12) The overwhelming majority of religions compel their followers to "work" their way toward reward. Islam, in particular, places exhaustive ritualistic demands of prayer and fasting upon its followers. But the Bible is clear in that the goodness of human beings falls short of God's glory. "There is none righteous, no, not one..." (Rom 3:10)

The defining characteristics of Christianity are numerous and varied, although Christianity and Judaism share a common history. Both faiths derive their belief of precious personhood from the Biblical account of creation found in the book of Genesis. "And the Lord God formed man of dust of the ground, and breathed into his nostrils the breath of life; and man became a living being." (Gen. 2:7) Scripture reveals that humanity did not evolve from lesser life forms, but was created just as we exist today - in the image of God. Our Heavenly Father lovingly and purposefully fashioned mankind in His image. The Bible makes abundantly clear that God's desire is to have fellowship with mankind. No other creation of God enjoys this privilege. The angels are created servants; humanity are God's children.

All life, and the human body especially, is a masterpiece of creation. The human brain alone not only produces our thoughts, emotions and coordinated physical actions, but also regulates the body's unconscious processes, such as breathing and digestion. Such a highly sophisticated and complex organ could not possibly have been the result of millennia of evolution of a single-celled organism, thrust into existence by galactic happenstance. Only a power far greater than anything in existence is capable of designing such a miraculous instrument, whose recipients do not yet fully grasp its unfathomable depths. Considering how our brains function at the cellular level, it becomes apparent how much the Lord truly loves us. He didn't have to create a brain that is capable of healing itself, whose regions compensate for another damaged area. How amazing is it that the human brain is practically infinite, that there is no limit to what we can learn? Humanity could have functioned, and thrived, with brains of lesser capacity, but God is so generous. The very same God who "...laid the foundations of the earth," (Job 38:4) designed the human brain. With all its amazing abilities, the human brain is an immense gift from a loving God to His beloved creation.

Christianity is also unique in that the dynamic Spirit of God indwells a believer, and imparts wisdom and guidance. "...Or do you not know that your body is the temple of the Holy Spirit who is in you, whom you have from God..." (1 Corinthians 6:19) The resulting loving, intimate, empowering relationship between God and believer creates a launch pad for miracles and change. "If you abide in Me, and My words abide in you, you will ask what you desire, and it shall be done for you." (John 15:7) And yet, it's interesting to note how much of the world views a life surrendered to Jesus Christ as dull and forbidding, because of the believer's abstention from many contemporary vices and panaceas. For the most part Christians don't dress too revealing or immodestly; avoid many R-rated movies containing gratuitous profanity, sexuality, and violence; practice fidelity in marriage; and engage in moderate consumption of alcohol – if at all. From the world's perspective, it appears that believers are missing out on all the good stuff in life. Oh, how wrong they are.

If what we are seeing of the contemporary world the best it has to offer, then it makes being a servant of Jesus Christ even more desirable. To know that our God is far more powerful than all the forces on the earth combined is astounding. It is also very reassuring. We never have to accept a doctor's negative prognosis, or allow others to determine how much we can accomplish, or define who we are. Believers serve the God of all creation, and He has no limits. Why should we? With faith anything is possible.

Admittedly, millions of believers around the world are facing persecution for their faith. But God has not abandoned them. In fact, missionaries report of more miracles manifesting among third world populations than in Western nations, because the people have a greater hunger for God. Their faith runs deep, because without God they don't have much. So they are willing to put everything on the line to see a move of God, and that kind of faith is honored by Heaven. Whereas, believers in the West have become accustomed to freedom and abundance. We live safe, privileged, comfortable lives, and that lethargy has even crept into the modern Church. Jesus stated in Matthew 19:24, "…it is easier for a camel to go through the eye of a needle than for a rich man to enter the Kingdom of God." Believers of free nations have taken their liberties for granted, and have not guarded them with diligence. And now we are experiencing the tragic results of our apathy.

It has long been believed that the business of politics was no place for good Christians. They are, after all, rough and tumble venues, and its participants have grown increasingly corrupt with the passage of time. But it was not always so. Early in our nation's history men of faith and virtue were the most popular choices to lead, and represent their constituents. So imperative was the presentation of a virtuous countenance, that the appearance of impropriety, or mere hint of a scandal, could cost a man his aspirations for public office. Those with political ambitions, but less than laudable proclivities, rigorously hid the sordid details of their personal lives from the public eye. What was once considered scandalous has now become mundane. The current political scene is a far cry from what our Founding Fathers established. The characteristic greed and debauchery of our national politics merely reflect the values of a society that has lost its moral compass. Politics has become a very dirty business, and the only hope for real change is to bring God back into the political discussion. And yet, the cry of "separation of church and state" is sounded at just the mention of a believer entering the political arena. With all the crime and corruption this country must contend, it's astonishing that seemingly intelligent people are more afraid of the changes a public servant could enact by mixing a little faith with his/her politics.

But there has been reluctance on the Church's part as well, to enter the political fray, and the consensus among Christians as to the Church's place in politics is divided. However, governance was a regular part of life for Christians in 18th and 19th century America. Why does the issue generate such heated debate now? We've seen how far disdain of politics has gotten the Church over the last century. God has been removed from most all public life, and our faith is now being criminalized, as a result of the Church's leaving the running of government to nonbelievers. But the hostile atmosphere in contemporary society toward the Church should not be a deterrent to exercising our constitutional right to govern. In fact, the survival of our nation depends upon it.

Since the days of ancient Israel God established leaders to rule over His people. History shows us that when a King served the Lord the nation and its people prospered. David is a perfect example of a King with a servant's heart. So devoted was David to the Lord, his expressions of unreserved love and need for God are evident throughout the Psalms. God said of David, "The Lord has sought for Himself a man after His own heart, and the Lord has commanded him to be commander over His people, because you (Saul) have not kept what the Lord commanded you." (1 Samuel 13:14) Alternatively, a betrayal of God by the King, such as Solomon - who turned to false gods later in life - meant division of the people, and dissolution of the kingdom through conquest by foreign powers. Could that happen in the United States today? All signs seem to indicate that the stage is being set for just that possibility.

A great deal of wisdom is required to govern judiciously. It seems wisdom is in short supply in our world though, especially in the realm of politics. Scripture stresses the importance of wisdom in all areas of life, and the subject of wisdom is mentioned over forty times in the book of Proverbs alone. The Lord is the source of all true wisdom, and He makes it available to every believer. Wisdom was in evidence at the creation of our Constitution and the Declaration of Independence. Abraham Lincoln employed divine wisdom in his agenda to abolish slavery. We were collectively a much wiser nation when we acknowledged God in all our ways, and made God's laws our laws. The secularists and separatists can't even begin to fathom the degree of divine wrath we court just in response to the 63 million+ slaughtered unborn, and the surrendering of our children to the dictates of the LGBTQ+ agenda. Indeed, our politics over the last century have put our nation on the "endangered species" list, and we continue to drink and be merry, unaware of the grave danger that awaits us if we continue down this path. "If My people, who are called by My name will humble themselves, and pray and seek My face, and turn from their wicked ways, then will I hear from Heaven, and will forgive their sin and will heal their land." (2 Chronicles 7:14) God will not tolerate this degree of wickedness forever....we are running out of time.

Genesis 12:3 states, "I will bless those who bless you, And I will curse him who curses you; And in you all families of the earth shall be blessed." Another reason for the affluence and security the United States has enjoyed for so long has been due to the safe refuge America has provided to persecuted people, and until recently, our steadfast alliance to the restored nation of Israel. At the end of WWII desolate Jews from all over the world united in their ancestral land, and in 1948 the U.N. voted to recognize Israel as an independent nation. Since that time Israel and the United States have shared a loyal bond of friendship, and a political alliance. God's hand of blessing has been firmly upon the United States, in no small part because of its loyalty to Israel, and to the Jewish people.

Believers versed in Scripture, and mindful of the atrocities perpetrated against the Jewish people time and again, recognize the extreme danger Israel faces today from a largely anti-Semitic world, a heavily Muslim-influenced U.N., and a future nuclear Iran. In fact, the plight of Israel is one of several crucial issues motivating the Church to rouse from its long slumber – a period during which much valuable ground had been surrendered to the godless, and an inordinate amount of damage had been done to our society. Tragically, as Christians abdicated more and more of their responsibility to govern this nation, normally characteristic American charity was not forthcoming toward the Jewish people in their greatest time of crisis - the Holocaust. Millions of innocent lives were tragically lost as a result. Little has been said of the many boatloads of desperate Jewish refugees turned away by the American State Department, and by other nations as well, as the Nazi "War Machine" raged. The abandonment of the besieged Jewish people at a time when consummate evil tyrannized the globe will stand in the annals of history as a chilling glimpse of a possible future America....one in which government will replace God.

Chapter 2
POLITICS AND
THE CHURCH

IN A MELTING POT LIKE THE UNITED STATES, THERE ARE MANY ETHNIC, religious and ideological groups jockeying for supremacy. Politicians often appeal to fringe groups with growing numbers of indoctrinated, in hopes of channeling the demographic advantage into votes. Pandering to these groups often results in the creation of laws in their favor, that aren't always in the best interests of the nation as a whole. For example, the current administration desires to grant citizenship to millions of illegal immigrants, ostensibly in the interest of goodwill and altruism. But one can easily deduce the huge advantage that many grateful new constituents will provide in the way of votes in future elections.

The United States of America, once a nation painfully divided by racism, has evolved over the years into a predominantly color-blind society of racial unity and integration. Into this arena of elevated conscience strode the first successful African-American candidate for president. Never in the history of the United States was there a more perfect time for the election of a black Commander in Chief. Unfortunately, the country was so elated by centuries of prayer and civil rights struggles culminating in the election of the first African-American president, that people closed their eyes and ears to the alarming actions and proclamations of this perceived messiah to "fundamentally transform" the nation. Virtually overnight, the newly-elected president's radical agenda manifested in the form of policy changes and rhetoric which drew lines of division between people of different economic classes, differing moral values, opposing party affiliations, and different races. Suddenly, those who opposed the President's policies for any reason were decried as racist. Progressive liberals, in lemming-like fashion, lined up behind President Obama defiantly, prepared to excoriate and demonize wealthy citizens, religious institutions, and moral and fiscal conservatives of every stripe. While he rubbed shoulders with the wealthy Hollywood elite and corporate moguls, Barack Obama repeatedly called for the top 1% of the nation's wealthiest to "pay their fair share." This battle cry was intentionally declared in favor of, and ecstatically received by many people of color, who continued to maintain a disproportionately higher rate of poverty than white Americans. The U.S. Bureau of the Census documented in 2010 that the poverty rate for African-American households was at 27.4%, Hispanics 26.6%, Asians 12.1%, and white households 9.9%. Fully understanding the dynamics and emotions surrounding the socioeconomic disparity between whites and minorities, Barack Obama strategically stoked the dying embers of racism, and a growing entitlement mentality, to create a Saul Alinsky style class war in contemporary America. With the help of loyal supporters who shared Obama's vision of communal utopia, and radically liberal cabinet members like the avowed Socialist Van Jones spouting incendiary refrains like "Give them the wealth," Obama's ideology resonated with many disillusioned young people and minorities, eager for an opportunity to level the economic playing field. As a result, bitter resentment toward society's more affluent increased among those who felt trapped in the lower economic brackets. This bitterness quickly translated into the rationale that since Caucasians held most of the wealth in the nation, everything associated with white America was inimical. In this highly-charged, politically correct atmosphere it was suddenly offensive to be a Caucasian, or espouse Judeo-Christian Biblical values, even though 79% of Black Americans in 2013 identified as Christians. As the former Superintendent of the Department of Public Instruction, Wisconsin Governor Tony Evers worked with VISTA (Volunteers In Service To America), and encouraged Caucasian students to wear white wristbands to serve as reminders of their white privilege. Before a House Appropriations subcommittee hearing in March 2011, Attorney General Eric Holder defended the Black Panthers who menaced voters outside a Pennsylvania polling station in 2008. He said, "... when you compare what people endured in the South in the 60s to try to get the right to vote for African Americans, and compare what people were subjected to there to what happened in Philadelphia...I think does a great disservice to people who put their lives on the line, who risked all for my people." By "my people" Mr. Holder was not referring to Americans, but only African-Americans.

Obama's America was at war – with itself. The media downplayed or under-reported incidents of minority violence against white people, or black-on-black crime, while simultaneously exaggerating, or in some cases distorting, the accounts of crimes committed by whites against minorities. In the Trayvon Martin case, several media outlets played fast and loose with the facts in their reporting. At first it was reported that a white man had "hunted down like a dog," according to Congresswoman Maxine Waters, a young, defenseless Trayvon Martin, then killed him in cold blood. As a result of the efforts of the more objective news outlets, the true facts slowly began to emerge. Even Trayvon's Christian mother, in an interview with Bill O'Reilly, disclosed truths about the death of her son that the mainstream media had misrepresented.

Barack Obama also made no secret of his loyalty to Islam, and many believed he put that loyalty ahead of the welfare of the United States. One example was the signing of the Kerry-Lugar bill in October of 2009, which allocated 7.5 billion dollars of non-military aid to Pakistan over

a five year period. The strategy behind this move was to ostensibly "…
combat extremism and anti-American sentiment…" And the controversy
continues over how much cash was delivered to Iran on numerous pallets,
supposedly releasing their own assets which had been frozen through
sanctions to impede their nuclear plan. This all transpired while the cost
of living was exploding in the U.S., and people were struggling to put
food on their tables. The average price of gas reached $3.83 per gallon in
2012, and remained high throughout Obama's presidency. The surreal
term "New Normal" epitomized the uncharacteristic lack and hardship
that the American people were experiencing for the first time in over
half a century.

To no one's surprise, the same scenario is playing out today in Biden's
administration, who no doubt is continuing his former boss's agenda.
"Lawlessness" now describes the Democrat party. Lawbreakers are no
longer jailed for their crimes, while in many U.S. cities innocent citizens
are instead prosecuted for defending themselves against criminal attacks.
The unprecedented numbers of illegal, unvetted immigrants allowed
entrance into this country has reached millions. Any reasonably sane
individual can imagine the horrific dangers these unknown invaders
pose to the safety and security of this country. And yet, the media and
many deceived people who continue to believe the lies and schemes of
the political class, proclaim all this violence and lawfare a healthy, vibrant
democracy. Meanwhile, the growing list of differences that separate us
are beginning to outnumber the qualities that should unite us all as
Americans.

Politics in this nation have become increasingly polarizing as
our society has moved closer and closer toward embracing a godless
worldview. The more hostility displayed toward Christians by
nonbelievers and secularists, the more the Church was galvanized as a
conservative group. But if conservatism became the direction American
Evangelicals and Fundamentalists alike were taking, the Democrat

Party did all but drive Christians away by attacking their Bible-based values. To Liberals, a pro-life belief and traditional marriage stance have become synonymous with hatred and intolerance. Christians who sided with Democrats for the working class principles they once professed to espouse, found themselves in a dilemma when forced to accept immoral values and legalized abortion on the same ticket as those principles. But many Christians shut their eyes to a political candidate's policies, because they lack a fundamental understanding of Scripture, and their ears are easily tickled by a politician's seducing words. People who justify such actions are only fooling themselves. God doesn't alter His laws because they've suddenly become unpopular or inconvenient. And we don't have to wonder if a candidate will uphold God's principles once in office; all we have to do is look at his/her track record, and associations. Jesus said, "You will know them by their fruits."(Matthew 7:16) When we choose the lesser of two evils, what we are left with is still evil.

As believers, we must submit to God's guidance in all areas of our lives. Experience should tell us that the areas in which God is not included ultimately yield pain and adversity. Politics are no exception. As our brother's keeper we cannot afford to depend upon those in whom the Holy Spirit does not dwell to make far-reaching decisions, and be responsible for the weak and vulnerable of this world. To the godless morality is relative. "Therefore, to him who knows to do good and does not do it, to him it is sin." (James 4:17) It's no secret that many politicians of different parties have been strongarmed, or blackmailed into complicity by wealthy criminals, and other politicians who have been corrupted. While I certainly have compassion for them with regard to the momentous decision each faces, to acquiesce is to be complicit in illegal dealings, drug and human trafficking, and the deaths of countless human beings. Would it not be better instead to walk away from a cherished political career, than to have innocent blood on one's hands? What a very sad commentary it is about our society that so many choose to enable death and human suffering on a scale never seen before in human history, rather than forfeit a little public acclaim or importance. Whatever amount of positive change these corrupted politicians might affect for their constituents, it will never come close to the degree of human suffering they make possible by partnering with evil.

This world is full of darkness, and it is the mission of the Body of Christ to bring light into the world. "Walk as children of light (for the fruit of the Spirit is in all goodness, righteousness, and truth), finding out what is acceptable to the Lord. And have no fellowship with the unfruitful works of darkness, but rather expose them." (Ephesians 5:8-11) Jesus bestowed the authority and the power of His shed blood upon no other people. God's Word is clear. Our task, challenging though it may be, lies before us. Therefore, if politics are designed to govern a nation, then something far greater must govern our politics.

JONAH AND THE WHALE

A little girl was talking to her teacher about whales. The teacher said it was physically impossible for a whale to swallow a human, because even though a whale is very large its throat is very small.

The little girl stated that Jonah was swallowed by a whale. Irritated, the teacher repeated that a whale could not swallow a human; that was physically impossible.

The little girl responded, "Well, when I get to Heaven, I will ask Jonah."

The teacher asked, "What if Jonah went to Hell?"

The little girl replied, "Then you ask him."

Author Unknown

Chapter 3
GOD'S WORD VS MAN'S LAW

A VERY STRAIGHTFORWARD, AND CONTROVERSIAL, COMMAND OF GOD'S IS Romans 13:1-2. "Let every soul be subject to the governing authorities. For there is no authority except from God, and those that exist have been appointed by God. Therefore whoever resists the authority resists the ordinance of God, and those who resist will bring judgment on themselves." This is an explicit command to obey our nation's laws, and any reasonable person can appreciate the benefits derived from an orderly society. But man's laws can often be contrary to the laws of God; abortion is a striking example. Thus, it should be remembered that God is above any earthly authority or law, and Christians must obey His will whatever the cost to themselves. The annual estimate of 6,000 people who are martyred worldwide for their faith know how much uncompromising obedience to God can cost a believer. (Statistic obtained from the advocacy group Open Doors' database) Christians must put God's laws above politics. God's Word should not be compromised. It is as relevant today as it was 2000 years ago.

When Jesus proclaimed "Therefore render to Caesar the things that are Caesar's, and to God the things that are God's," (Matt 22:21) did He intend for His followers to surrender a brother or sister to the authorities if they were breaking the law in some way? Does subjection to the governing authorities, as spoken of in Romans 13, mean to place obedience of the law above the welfare of another? If one has knowledge of a believer's illegal status, is it their Christian, as well as civic duty, to report him? What does it say about one's faith in God to protect His own, if a believer does not report his brother to the authorities, but continues instead to shelter him illegally? Doing so technically makes him an accomplice to a crime, but is he guilty of disobeying God's Word as well? Discerning God's will under such conflicting circumstances can be a challenge, and there are more Scriptures in support of obeying the law than there are for going against it. However, in most passages of Scripture the "law" referred to is God's law, not the secular law instituted by governments. Oftentimes, Christians find themselves on the wrong side of a nation's law by virtue of their beliefs. Martyrdom is achieved by disobedience to the law. Technically, it may be said that Jesus was in violation of Hebraic law - as interpreted by the Scribes, when He claimed to be the Messiah. The fact that it was true didn't matter to the Pharisaical leaders of His time, who brooked no transgression of the Law they decreed, especially when it could result in upsetting their comfortable way of life.

With full acknowledgement of Romans 13, it must be said that lawmakers are human and fallible, and some of their laws are flawed. When laws are created by a godless ruling body, disobedience to the law is often not only required of a Christian, but necessary. Should not God's commands be upheld under any and all circumstances? Or should a believer obey all the laws of the land in which he/she resides? Should a Christian woman in China comply with the law, and abort her unborn child? What should a believer do when his Christian faith violates the law of his land, and marks him an infidel and a criminal?

The most interesting fact about Romans 13 is that the very government the Apostle Paul was urging obedience to by the Church, was the very government that was putting Christians to death. The Bible makes it clear that believers should not lie to escape death for their faith, as a martyr's death emulates our Savior's, and is the highest glory for a believer. Further, it is a powerful witness to others, and a demonstration of complete surrender to God. "And they stoned Stephen as he was calling on God and saying, 'Lord Jesus, receive my spirit.' Then he knelt down and cried out with a loud voice 'Lord, do not charge them with this sin.' And when he had said this, he fell asleep." (Acts 7:59-60) God can accomplish much in the world through such a powerful testimony. But if a believer conceals another from danger, is he saying by his actions that he has no faith in God? Do his actions indicate he does not believe God can protect the condemned, or that death cannot be part of the Father's perfect plan? If someone shields another from imprisonment or death, is he being disobedient to God, as well as the authorities under who's rule he lives?

Several years ago a family who had sought religious asylum in the United States joined the congregation of a Minnesota church. The family of four had escaped religious persecution in Afghanistan, and was living illegally in hiding with a Minneapolis family. Their circumstances were known initially by only a few people in their church, and almost everyone who knew wanted to be of help to the refugee family. But after several months, a well-respected couple who had a long history of membership with the church, decided that they could no longer continue to have knowledge of an illegal situation without acting. They viewed their decision to report the refugee family to the Department of Immigration as the lawful, and Christian thing, to do.

The father was the first to be deported, even though he, his wife, and several of their American friends had pleaded with the authorities, and argued strenuously that to return him to his country could mean his execution. His wife was deported a month later, but their two teenaged daughters managed to evade custody, and several months later were still living on the run. Needless to say, much controversy and division was stirred up in the church over the actions of the couple who had reported the Afghani family to the authorities. Most congregants were shocked and outraged over the couple's lack of compassion, knowing how dire the family's situation was. But the couple was adamant that dishonesty was wrong in all cases, and those who were withholding information about the refugee family's whereabouts were guilty of sin, in addition to breaking the law. Most church members who knew about the family's plight felt it was wrong to send people to their possible deaths - especially a brother or sister in the Lord - no matter the circumstances. They believed that to protect the family was the compassionate and Godly thing to do, even if it meant lying to the authorities. The refugee family's plight was compared to that of the Jews in Nazi Germany. It can safely be said that there was no doubt the people who protected the Jews from the Nazis during World War II were doing the right thing in the eyes of the Judeo-Christian world at the time. But other members of the Minneapolis church argued it was wrong to break the law, and cited many verses of Scripture as justification, in particular Hebrews 13:17. "Obey those who rule over you, and be submissive, for they watch out for your souls, as those who must give an account." They maintained that to break the law is indicative of a lack of faith that God can protect His own, even under the most threatening and seemingly hopeless conditions.

The fates of the Afghani father and mother were still not known two years later, nor were the whereabouts of their daughters. This was a heartbreaking situation that served to expose the weak links in that church, and possibly within the Body of Christ. The fault does not lie with Scripture's vastness of meaning, but with believers' lack of surrender to God. When believers are truly surrendered to the Lord, it is His will they seek, and not their own. When believers are truly surrendered to the Lord, the Holy Spirit will illuminate deeper meaning of a passage of Scripture, and guide us into the perfect will of God. Therefore, it should be clear to believers to take no action against another unless they have a clear directive from the Lord. If there is the slightest doubt, they should do nothing, except pray and intercede. It is all too easy for people's emotions and personal biases to get in the way and color their thinking, as well as their faiths. Oftentimes people will decide on a course of action, then search the Scriptures for verses to justify their position. Wars have been started this way. If members of the Minneapolis church believed what the Afghani family was doing was wrong, then they should have spoken to the family, and urged them to comply with the law. Had the situation escalated to the point where the refugee family was openly flaunting disobedience to the laws of their host country, then in compliance with Scripture, the family might have been asked to leave the church. Was the couple who reported the family devout Christians sincerely expressing obedience to God by obeying the law? Or were they average people who subconsciously felt elated at the rare prospect of wielding power over others? Only God truly knows their hearts.

Choosing to disobey the law may seem as though someone doesn't have enough faith in the Lord to entrust the welfare of imperiled people to His loving hands. But even with a mountain of faith, it would have been excruciatingly difficult to surrender that family to the authorities to be deported, and possibly executed. Many devout believers, if asked by authorities if they had any knowledge of the family's whereabouts, would have lied. They would have done the same for endangered Jews in Nazi Germany, and their faith would never have been questioned.

In the book of Joshua, Rahab's lie to the King of Jericho to protect the Hebrew spies earned her a place in the lineage of Jesus. After Abram presented his wife Sarai to the Pharoah of Egypt as his sister, in fear for his life, the Lord blessed him and made him the father of a great nation. These examples make one wonder if God takes into consideration extenuating circumstances. Does He measure the weightiness of the possible outcome for telling the truth against a well-intentioned lie? Does the principle of Romans 8:28 apply in those situations? "And we know that for those who love God all things work together for good, for those who are called according to His purpose." Or in God's eyes, does accomplishing a greater good render a lie not a sin? Are there degrees of sin in lying, depending upon the gravity of the consequences for telling the truth?

God is perfect, but this world is not. God's laws should not be in question, but governments and their laws. Not all man-made laws are designed in the best interest of the people they are created to protect, and citizens should not be bound by laws that conflict with their deeply held faiths. Christian parents in Europe and the United States have been fined, and some jailed for spanking their children, even though the Bible is clear that it is a prescribed method of discipline. "Do not withhold correction from a child; for if you beat him with a rod, he will not die." (Proverbs 23:13) Some pastors continue to speak God's Word from the pulpit, even when it is in opposition to the law of the land. Pastors in many countries have been imprisoned for countering homosexuality and abortion with Scripture. Many law-abiding Christians have been arrested for blocking abortion clinic entrances; they believed that to allow the bodies of the unborn to be savagely destroyed would be a far greater sin than breaking the law.

It must be acknowledged that man's law will frequently oppose God's law, and the Godly will face tough decisions. Of course, there are natural limits in practicing one's faith, and that is where it infringes upon the rights of others to live their lives as they choose. Lawlessness should never be advocated. But those who make the laws are people with an agenda, and all too often that agenda is contrary to God's, and harmful to believers. This calls for discernment on the part of every citizen, especially Christians. People, including believers, must be very careful to guard against taking matters into their own hands, and declaring it God's will.

THE OASIS OF HIS PRESENCE

Here, in the glorious presence of the Lord,

I am free from all strife, and can melt into His arms.

What a relief it is to completely shut out the world for a while,

and breathe in the Holy Spirit.

Thank you Father, for this respite.

Thank you for Your attention, and for your time.

What a joy and a privilege it is to hear You speak to me.

You tell me of Your love and Your faithfulness,

Your promise to never leave me, nor turn a deaf ear to

my pleas.

You reveal to me how much my praise and declarations

of love mean to You,

And I am overcome by that revelation.

You ask for so little in return for all You give.

It is so hard to end my times with you,

And return to the cold, hard, loud, threatening place the

world has become.

But I can bear it, because Your Spirit strengthens me.

Nevertheless, I look toward the day when I will rejoice in the

light of Your glorious presence without end.

Rosalie Gilliland

Chapter 4
THE EMERGING CHURCH IN AMERICA

THERE IS A GROWING MOVEMENT TODAY IN THE AMERICAN CHURCH THAT HAS
the potential to undermine the Church's influence through ideological
division. The Emerging Church is responding to a rapidly changing
culture by practicing the way of Jesus within a *Postmodern* society, as
each group and individual within the movement interprets it. Essentially,
what this movement purports to do is return Christian-style living back
to first century Christianity. How exactly this is done, and what it looks
like, varies by group and region.

Postmodernism is difficult to define, as there is no absolute consensus
among postmodern thinkers. It is essentially a rejection of the late 19th
and early 20th centuries' move by the Roman Catholic and Protestant
churches, to interpret the teachings of the Bible through the lens of
intellectual reasoning and current knowledge. (Theological Modernism).
After centuries of Church domination, religious wars, death, division and
chaos, Europe was hungry for change. Out of the ashes of unquestioned
authority and tradition arose the desire for truth that only reason,
observation and experiment could meet. The 18th century gave birth
to a new Europe - one of reason, and the philosopher and the scientist
replaced the Catholic and Protestant Church hierarchies as the experts

on the meaning of life. After a century of scientific advancement, people couldn't help but compare the progress of science with that of the ruling Church, where the same dialogue that was out of touch with the needs of the masses continued unabated. As the new philosophical thinking, Modernism motivated people of all classes to question their inherited beliefs.

But Postmodernism brought down the walls erected around Modernism's science and reason that had kept them separate from, and superior to, the school of faith. Faith and reason were now united in a new dialogue, and what was expelled was the age-old enemy of faith - cynicism. Postmodernism recognizes that humanity has a deeply entrenched need for the things that cannot be explained, but are strongly felt. Experiences like love, the beauty of nature, acts of kindness, and worship nurture the longings of the human heart. Postmodernism created a climate in which those longings are validated.

However, if there is one area in which Modernism and Postmodernism radically differ, it is in Postmodernism's denial that Scripture is objectively and authoritatively true. Postmodernism takes a subjective approach to Scripture, and places a greater emphasis on personal spirituality and experience. The Emerging Church immerses itself in the concept of involvement as the vehicle needed to engage contemporary culture, and save souls. And whereas the Modernist Church engaged in philosophical discussion on ways to improve the plight of the suffering masses, the Postmodernists are actually out in the streets making it happen.

The nation actually saw the stirrings of postmodernism in the 1950s. With the end of the Second World War, the United States experienced a shift in traditional values. After working outside the home, many women were reluctant to return to the role of homemaker, and sought more independence. Means of travel were vastly improved over pre-war days, and more people were leaving the farms and small towns in which they had grown up. The world was on the move, and this restlessness was felt in every facet of society. The Church was no exception. As more people began to openly question whether traditional values and morality were even relevant anymore, church attendance began to gradually decline. Seduced by postmodern philosophy, congregants began to require their church's beliefs and practices conform to reach a new, postmodern world.

The Jesus Movement of the 1970s ushered in a new era of freedom in worship, which until then only a few sects within the Pentecostal Church had ever experienced. Many new believers joined the trendy movement because it was hip and unique. Others, disillusioned by the emptiness of the new consumerism resulting from a booming post-war economy, came to the movement seeking inner fulfillment. This new movement brought people of different races and socio-economic groups together in worship. That was a new concept, and a timely one, in a rapidly changing American landscape.

The Emerging Church movement is still a relatively new one, and no standard of how to "do" Church has yet been established. The driving sentiment among the Emerging Church is to get as far away from religion as possible. In fact, the trend among church planters is to avoid anything at all that bears semblance to any institution. For the last several decades, new churches have been springing up in urban areas all around the country. Pews were pulled out, and replaced with folding chairs, floor mats and couches. Church services are held in rented buildings, members' apartments, basements, and any accommodations available. In the spirit of first century Christianity, a service can be as simple as members sharing a meal, singing hymns, and reading Scripture. Serving others is emphasized as much as worship, and it is common for Emergents to be out in their communities ministering to the residents. Given the fact that many urban areas are financially depressed, justice has become a major focus among Emerging Church members. The driving passion of the Emerging Church is to bring Jesus to those who might not otherwise hear God's love story to humanity. For that cause, members of the movement suffer the disdain of mainline denominations, and the poverty that is often the result of breaking away from a larger denomination that has buckled under political or social pressure to compromise their doctrine.

Emergents' zeal for spreading the Gospel, at least as they interpret it, cannot be denied. Many urban areas host new churches planted by people who believe that God has called them into an unfamiliar and challenging wilderness. Their wilderness can be a drug-ridden neighborhood, whose residents ran out of hope a long time ago. Or it can be a poor community of predominantly single parent households. The children in that neighborhood need to hear that they have a Father who loves them, and who will never leave them. Church planters improvise and make do with whatever they can get their hands on to bring "church" to people who wouldn't normally attend church. In their unique way they are fulfilling the Great Commission.

For all the things it is not, there is a general consensus among its members on what the Emerging Church is, and its mission. In their book, *Emerging Churches: Creating Christian Community in Postmodern Cultures,* Eddie Gibbs and Ryan Bolger define the movement by nine characteristics. "Emerging churches (1) identify with the life of Jesus (2) transform the secular realm (3) live highly communal lives (4) welcome the stranger (5) serve with generosity (6) participate as producers (7) create as created beings (8) lead as a body (9) take part in spiritual activities." (Baker Publishing Group, Grand Rapids, MI: 2005) These are all Biblical mandates, and practiced by well-known and respected Christian ministers, such as former Cornerstone Community Church Pastor and founder of Crazy Love Ministries, Francis Chan. Pastor Chan and his family left their suburban home to live in a depressed, urban California neighborhood, bringing Jesus into the streets to minister to the prostitutes and drug dealers. Taking their faith to a level that leaves many believers quaking in their boots, the Chan family routinely welcomes street people to share their home, as they transition from individuals in crisis to Kingdom dwellers. But this is not how Emerging Church life always looks. Because of the wide range of translating the nine characteristics of the movement, the differences between churches can be night and day.

There are many factors that influence a new church, such as church affiliation, ordination of the church leader, the gender of the church leader, and the church's vision. Affiliation with a mainstream denomination may translate into better finances for a newly planted church, but it also means adherence to a church doctrine that the Emergents may not completely embrace. New churches that go it alone are completely dependent upon the Lord for provision. To make ends meet, members utilize whatever meeting space they can afford in which to hold services. This usually means arriving hours before to set up, and breaking down and storing all the seating and equipment afterward. The Pastor often has a regular job outside the church, and contributions of money, food, supplies and furniture are always welcome. Church members often pool their talents to start small businesses, and any profits are channeled into the operation of their church. Creativity is an asset in church planting, as are faith and patience.

Not all new Emerging churches survive. There are currently no statistics available on the number of new churches that don't last. But surveys conducted over the last decade by organizations like Pew Forum reveal that Christians' allegiance to traditional denominations is declining, while membership in Pentecostal churches is on the rise. "According to various scholars and sources, Pentecostalism - a Protestant Christian movement - is the fastest growing religion in the world. This growth is primarily due to religious conversion. According to the Pulitzer Center, 35,000 people become Pentecostal or 'Born Again' every day." (www.pewresearch.org) This trend reflects a move away from mainline denominations toward less traditional churches.

The Emerging Church movement is growing and gaining momentum, so they must be doing something right. The community engagement efforts of the Emerging Church are making a noticeable difference, as many historically low-income neighborhoods across the country are being revitalized. The Emerging Church is doing more than saving souls. With their inviting early Church style of ministry, they are saving whole communities. But because the tenets of the Emerging Church movement are not explicitly defined, they remain open to interpretation. This fact, combined with the Emerging Church's drive to distance itself from traditional church, can sometimes result in a loose and liberal interpretation of Scripture. But if the absolute truth of God's Word is not unconditionally upheld, then truth becomes relative. When the truth is relative, what meaning do Christ's death and resurrection have?

Veering into the territory of heresy is one of the dangers facing the Emerging Church, who desire above all to be inclusive. Adherence to the ideal of inclusion by well-meaning believers can lead to "Ecumenism," defined by dictionary.com as "The principle or aim of promoting unity among the world's Christian Churches." If Scripture is open to subjective interpretation, and there is no specific guiding theology, then Salvation can theoretically be interpreted by a new convert as whatever he/she wants it to be. It's not uncommon for new Emergent believers to accept Jesus Christ, while retaining some of their former religion's or belief system's doctrines, picking and choosing the tenets from each they wish to preserve. In fact, one particular movement has emerged recently, whereby adherents stand on the principle that God accepts people just as they are. Initially, this is true, because everyone has sinned. But Jesus died to absolve all humanity from sin, and when people receive Jesus as Lord and Savior, they must acknowledge and surrender all sin in their lives. Repentance means a sincere conviction of sin, and a turning away from it. The Bible is not ambiguous about sin. And only those who don't want to see the truth will distort the Word of God, and declare their sin accepted by Him, and therefore righteous. And that is a very dangerous illusion to embrace.

The influence of contemporary society cannot be discounted, as most good people are hyper-conscious not to offend those who embrace different ideologies. This paradox can put a burden on members of the Emerging Church to compromise God's truth *just enough* so as not to offend a "seeker." While it may be necessary to search out new ways to witness to a changing culture, employing dialogue which "waters down" or compromises the truth of the Gospel will only lead to false doctrine. This will ultimately establish a new believer on a weak foundation, leaving him/her defenseless against influence by demonic forces.

Despite the faith and devotion of many in the Emerging Church movement, and its record of leading countless people to Jesus and improving their lives, its members have been described as little more than culture warriors. The Emerging Church's passionate focus on championing society's poor, combined with a *relative truth* concept that infiltrates the faith of many of the movement's members, often results in a rather morally relativistic worldview. Thus, some of the Emerging Church's members embrace a liberal political ideology, in hopes of attaining a more equitable society. Whether these individuals actually believe abortion and same-sex marriage are acceptable in the eyes of the Lord, or tolerate them as concessions to attaining a greater societal good, only God knows. Support of this ideology by some of the Emerging Church's members is another reason the movement finds itself at odds with the majority of Pentecostal churches.

Emergents believe that the Church needs to change to survive, and view the Emerging Church movement as "Post-Evangelical" *(a new interpretation of Evangelicalism)*. This concept manifests in a number of ways, the most significant being that much of the Emerging Church tends to be unaccepting of Systematic Theology. They don't embrace a single, "air-tight" statement of faith, but rather the truth of salvation in Christ alone is open to interpretation. As can be expected, Evangelical

Christians are alarmed by this loose theology, and how perilously close it approaches heresy.

Ultimately, the Emerging Church is committed to transforming the Body of Christ, and compares its task in importance to what was accomplished by the Jesus Movement of the 1970s. Even though there is some overlap in beliefs among Emergents and more moderate Evangelicals, each side is committed to its theology, and so repelled by the other's, that the Church is somewhat weakened by this division. Tragically, the secular element of our society is encouraged by this separation among believers, to push their godless agenda through a void left by a torn Church.

LIVE LIKE YOU'RE DYING

"Prefiero morir de pie que vivir de las rodillas." (I prefer to die on my feet than live on my knees).

-Emiliano Zapata

"During times of universal deceit, telling the truth becomes a revolutionary act."

-George Orwell

"The greatest glory in living lies not in never falling, but in rising every time we fall."

- Nelson Mandela

"The only thing necessary for the triumph of evil is for good men to do nothing."

- Sir Edmund Burke

"A nation which can prefer disgrace to danger is prepared for a master, and deserves one."

- Alexander Hamilton

"Courage is not simply one of the virtues, but the form of every virtue at the testing point."

-C.S. Lewis

"Eternal vigilance is the price of liberty."

-Thomas Jefferson

"Those who would surrender essential liberty for temporary security, will in the end deserve neither liberty nor security."

-Benjamin Franklin

Chapter 5

WHAT WAS MEANT
FOR EVIL

THE FACE OF HOME SCHOOLING HAS CHANGED DRAMATICALLY SINCE LEFTIST
thinkers such as Ivan Illich, Paul Goodman and A.S. Neill promoted
a new movement of "unschooling" as a revolt against standardized
education. Since then, the movement has increased to approximately
3.7 million home-schooled students in the United States, according to
the National Home Education Research Institute (NHERI). In earlier
years, religion was the main reason parents homeschooled their children.
They opposed many of the influences their children were subjected to
in public schools, which have metastasized in recent years to downright
dangerous and disturbing. But many families have opted out of public
education for reasons other than religion. The public school system has
failed our children miserably. Many public schools have all but ceased
to teach standard academics, but are now tampering with children's
minds by forcing progressive ideology on them. Gender confusion and
personal pronouns have replaced science, English and math are regarded
as racially bigoted subjects, and history has either been rewritten or
completely discarded. Most inner city schools have become war zones,
and children are in danger of gang and gun violence. Parents who could
afford it removed their children from these houses of horrors. But the

majority of parents with children in failing public schools don't have the same options. Private school is unaffordable, and there are too few Charter schools. Most parents would like nothing more than to remove their children from these failing institutions, but it simply is not possible for most single, or financially struggling parents. Others, for a variety of reasons, are not able to school their children in academic subjects. It seemed like the future for many unfortunate children had already been decided. Then Covid happened.

The world was ordered to shut themselves in their homes for 2 weeks, to "flatten the curve" of some mysterious disease. Children were provided online lessons to complete, and it all seemed easy enough. But then 2 weeks turned into an indeterminate amount of time, as a vaccine was supposedly being formulated to battle a disease no one knew anything about. Now parents were expected to tutor their children in their lessons, whether or not they were able. And what a surprise the arrogant U.S. Board of Education unveiled to unprepared parents in the form of their children's school curriculum.

Suddenly, parents had full view of the filth and insanity that was being foisted upon their children in the name of education. More attention was being paid to gender and race issues than academics. In twenty first century America, children were being taught that people of color were racially oppressed, and white people - including children, were their oppressors. Sexuality was being addressed even in lower elementary grade classes. Students were being taught that there are more than two genders, and a person can change their gender whenever they want. Many elementary schools continue to welcome drag queens to conduct Story Hour to young children. To say that parents were stunned by all this insanity is an understatement. "When in the world did this happen," they asked themselves, "and how did we miss it?" Almost overnight, it seemed that public school had turned into a horror show. Decisions were made never to return a child to those dangerous environments again.

Now, parents who previously didn't think it possible, were determined to find a way to home school their children. Many neighborhoods coalesced into strategic groups, assigning one parent to teach one subject, another parent to teach another subject. Working single parents who couldn't spare the time to home school, were able to conduct field trips. Everyone worked together, and actively participated in their children's education. Remarkably, some families found this new way of schooling effectively improved their family dynamic. Many families report that the quality time spent in pursuit of a common purpose has drawn families, and communities, closer together. In fact, more than a few have claimed this chapter in their lives to be the best thing that has ever happened to their families.

Home schooling's flexibility offers many benefits. First and foremost among them is the students' safety. Not only are children physically safer than in some dangerous public school environment, but exposure to attitudes hostile to their religious beliefs is avoided. In fact, religion is often part of the curriculum. The "media and mall" influence is also reduced. The flexible schedule enables students to participate in many activities public schools may not offer, due to dwindling financial resources. Some of these activities include sports, dance, volunteerism, and also real-world experience, like operating a small business or learning a trade. Experimenting with educational innovation is possible thanks to technology, and a burgeoning cottage industry that provides books, materials and assistance of all kinds to home educators.

Contrary to popular opinion, home schooled students are friendlier, more independent, and more socially developed than their peers attending public or private schools. They also have higher self-esteem. These are the findings of the Fraser Institute, a public policy organization in Vancouver, British Columbia. Claudia Hepburn, former Director of Education policy stated, "Popular belief holds that home schooled children are socially backward and deprived, but research shows the opposite: that home schooled children are actually better socialized than their peers. These benefits may come from having parents, rather than peers, as primary behavior models." Research also reveals that home schooling families are actually more involved in their communities than public school families. They're more likely, for example, to have voted in the previous five years, participated in a community-service activity, or gone to the public library. In fact, home schooled students are involved in an average of 5 outside activities per week.

But home schooling continues to have its critics, and draw a great deal of controversy. Detractors claim that the Dept. of Education's budget is negatively impacted by the loss of revenue. But the truth is the principal source of revenue for public education is derived from property taxes. In fact, many states now count home schooled children in public-educational, per-student funding formulas. Opponents to home schooling contend students are receiving inferior educations. They just don't believe it's possible for students to get a quality education outside a traditional setting. But studies have shown that thinking to be biased, and far from the truth. The most extensive study conducted on the subject to date, is a 103-page peer reviewed journal published in 2004 by Brian Ray, President of the Salem, OR National Home Education Research Institute. The findings reveal that home schoolers are frequently top achievers, scoring higher than the national average on standardized achievement tests. By the 8th grade home schooled students perform 4 grade levels above the national average. In addition, home schooled students tend to score significantly higher on standardized college entrance tests. Many researchers believe this is due, at least in part, to the individualized attention home educated students receive. Most selective colleges have no hesitation in admitting home schoolers, and many students have gained entry to elite universities such as Harvard, Yale, MIT and UC Berkeley. In fact, college admissions officers now recruit at home school conventions and conferences. Time will tell if this trend will continue now that DEI and Critical Race Theory strongly influence the decision making of many institutions - educational and other.

Critics also claim that home schooling is a religious phenomenon, but only 49% of home schooling parents identify as Evangelical Christians. Evangelicals who, unlike Catholics, did not have a school system of their own, were particularly impacted by public school environments hostile to their religious beliefs. Certainly deeply religious parents seek to shelter their children from many aspects of an increasingly immoral popular culture, and disapprove of the peer culture that is profoundly influential in public and private schools. Now these parents have a viable option for successfully educating their children, without all the negative factors encountered in public and private schools.

Home schooling has certainly come a long way since the days when home educators were engaged in heated battles with local school districts and state lawmakers for the right to exist. Home schooling is now legal in every state, and the results demonstrate that parents are doing a stellar job. Now that home schooling families have won the battle for legitimacy, they are shifting their emphasis toward redefining educational excellence, and producing well-educated, responsible citizens prepared for the challenges of the 21st century.

Chapter 6
MY FIRST ENCOUNTER
WITH CHRISTIANS

I ONCE WORKED, AND WAS FRIENDS WITH, A YOUNG CHRISTIAN WOMAN BY THE name of Maddie. Maddie and I were both employed with an insurance company in the mid-seventies, and we worked in an office with several other young women. Being a devout Kingdom servant, Maddie lived her faith openly, and witnessed to others at every opportunity. I was one of the hapless heathens Maddie witnessed to, and on one particular occasion my response to her attempt to save my soul was less than laudable.

Each of the young women in our section of the office came to be identified by our most outstanding characteristics or proclivities. Rona, being a married mother and a little older than the rest of us, was "Mom." She always had a willing ear for her single co-workers and our problems, and offered sound, sensible advice. Valerie, with her wild dark hair, eccentric clothes, and even more eccentric lifestyle, was the Bohemian artist. Long before the Vegan diet had become popular, Valerie abstained from unhealthy fare, eating foods the rest of us had never even heard of. She certainly was ahead of her time. Becky was an innocent Mid-Western girl from South Dakota, who would blush at everything. Living in the big, bad city of San Diego, CA gave Becky a lot to blush over. We often wondered how she would have fared in a place like Las Vegas. As the

Senior Administrator, Sheila was our boss, and the corporate ladder-climber. She was a devoted employee, and planned a long, aspiring career with the company. But when she got around the rest of us, our boss was as silly and chatty as a schoolgirl, making it hard for us to view her as an authority figure. Maddie was the Christian. Even in the 1970s, a Christian stood out from the crowd by virtue of his/her faith. Maddie was a Proverbs 31 woman, with not a drop of makeup, and very modest clothing. A natural beauty, Maddie's translucent light blue eyes were bright, and the kindest eyes I have ever seen. She was a very sweet, loving young woman, with a genuine smile and a soft voice. Then, there was me. I was the party girl, spending my nights twirling on the dance floor of every San Diego nightclub - or discotheque - as they were called in the seventies. Having fully bought into contemporary society's prescription for happiness, I was the typical young, suburban woman. I lived for little more than the spotlight, fashion, and the possibility of romance.

Maddie was very open about her faith, and if the other girls were bothered by it they never let it show. But neither did they display any interest in being saved. For some reason though, Maddie felt a real burden for me, and would frequently engage me in conversation, asking me questions about God to which I had no answers. Thus it was due to my inability to nimbly avoid getting roped into a more momentous assembling of the Saints, that I found myself at Maddie's apartment one evening, a reluctant guest at a modest meal and a three-pronged attack on my lifestyle. Maddie and her two roommates teamed up, and literally quoted chapter and verse to me. I had no knowledge of the Bible at the time, so I was in no position to debate their assertions. I politely agreed with their statements, as I did believe in God, but that was as far as I was prepared to allow their ambush to go. I had no intention of becoming one of them. I was an average, backslidden Roman Catholic, and I trotted out my piety every Christmas and Easter, just like any other normal person. Although I loved Jesus, I was not about to join the ranks of the "Jesus

Fanatics." No, I would just go along with their surprise intervention, and get out of that apartment as quickly, and with as little drama as possible. This I did, but on the drive home I could not shake the feeling that something had happened to me. Now some inexplicable sense of conviction had become my constant companion. This new development, of course, made me angry, as it would not be so easy now to pursue my carefree lifestyle. What I also experienced was a sense of sadness, but I could not understand why at the time. I just wanted to continue as I had before, and be like all the other happy young people living life to the fullest, unencumbered by conscience.

Shortly after my visit with Maddie and her roommates, my other co-workers were intensely curious to know how the visit went. By this time I was no longer capable of spending my nights in thoughtless pursuit of frivolous pleasure, and I was not happy about it. So I unloaded on my eager listeners, and I went too far. Maddie was not in the office at that moment, so I took full advantage of her absence, and maligned and ridiculed her and her roommates. "Born again?" I popped off, fancying myself a standup comic. "As if once is not enough!" My co-workers' howls of laughter fueled my performance, and it escalated to the point where I said some of the unkindest things about Maddie, her roommates, Christians in general, and God. Several minutes into my diatribe, I could tell by my co-workers' faces that someone was standing behind me, and somehow I just knew it was Maddie. I turned to see a look of pain on her saintly face that I will never forget, and which haunted me for years afterward. But to her credit, Maddie turned and walked quietly away, and we never spoke of this incident, or God, again.

I lasted only a few more months at that company, then tried my hand at other occupations, and marriage, unsuccessfully. All the while God was calling me, and I did my best to shut out His voice, until that was no longer possible. On November 2, 1979, led by a dear new friend and neighbor, Kerry, I gave my heart and life to Jesus Christ. But the memory of what I had done to Maddie continued to gnaw at me. I felt that I could not have complete peace until I had made things right with her. But several years had passed, and given the circumstances under which we parted, we had not stayed in touch. I prayed that God would grant me the grace to find Maddie, so I could apologize to her, and tell her that I was now a believer. I needed her to know that what she did for me had not been in vain. I began my search for Maddie by calling people we used to work with. Then I called people who knew her, then I called people who knew someone who knew her. Finding a person in the days before the internet was no easy task, but eventually I was successful.

The morning I planned to call Maddie had arrived, and I was so nervous. "Would she remember me?" I wondered, then realized that what I had done to her undoubtedly made me hard to forget. "What if she hangs up on me, or tells me off?" I thought to myself, panic starting to set in. That would really be awkward, but who could blame her if she did? All the possibilities of how Maddie might react raced through my mind, but I finally decided that I had to do this no matter what, and let come what may. So I summoned the courage to dial Maddie's phone number, and instantly recognized her gentle voice at the other end of the line. I could barely find my own voice to respond, but I managed to squeak out, "The Lord keeps His promises," in reference to Philippians 1:6. "...being confident of this very thing, that He who has begun a good work in you will complete it until the day of Jesus Christ..." There was a pause, then Maddie chuckled and replied sweetly, "He certainly does." I then revealed who it was that was calling her with such a strange message. To my relief and surprise she not only remembered me, but was happy to hear from me. As I was a new believer, it would be years before I came to realize that Maddie's gracious and forgiving response was typical of a servant of Christ. But on that memorable morning, Maddie rose greatly in my estimation, just as a result of that single noble act.

Maddie and I talked for quite a while. We shared the news that we were both married, and mothers of baby boys, approximately the same age. I told her that God had sent person after person into my life to witness to me. They were watering the seed that she had planted in me years before, for which I was very grateful. Finally a lull in the conversation provided the opportune moment to confess to Maddie how sorry I was for having said those hurtful things about her that day in the office, years before. To my amazement Maddie dismissed the matter, saying she had forgotten about it, and that my response had not been all that unusual anyway. "Anger is a common reaction when sinners are faced with the truth about God, and themselves" she said. I was stunned by her comment, but immensely relieved that I had been forgiven. Forgiveness is a huge gift – to both the forgiven, and the forgiver. After the conversation wound down, Maddie and I said our goodbyes and agreed that we should get together sometime, but it never happened. We were in two very different places in life. She, a long-time believer, was happily married to a Godly man and very settled. But my life at that time was the result of my experiences and incredibly bad choices. I was trapped in an unhappy, volatile marriage. Thus it was a struggle for me to grow as a Christian. It would be many more years before I experienced victory over my circumstances, and my flesh.

But every journey begins with a single step. The first step on my journey to salvation began when a loving, selfless girl opened her heart and her home to me, which would eventually lead me to Christ. It seemed only right that Maddie know this. And it was critical that I tell her - as much, if not more, for myself as for her.

THE TWELVE DAYS OF CHRISTMAS

This popular Christmas carol harkens back to Medieval England. The twelve days referenced in the song is the period between December 25 and the Epiphany, popularly believed when the Magi visited the Baby Jesus. Interestingly, before the carol became a staple of Western holiday tradition, the catchy ditty was frequently sung in English taverns.

My True Love is a reference to God. **A Partridge** is a coded reference to Jesus, as the partridge will feign injury to lure predators away from its nest, sacrificing its own life to protect its young. The **Pear Tree** represents the Cross. **The Two Turtle Doves** represent the Old and New Testaments. **The Three French Hens** stood for faith, hope and love. **The Four Calling Birds** represent the four Gospels, and the **Five Golden Rings** symbolize the Torah – the first five books of the Old Testament, which chronicle man's fall from grace. **The Six Geese a-laying** stand for the six days of creation. **The Seven Swans A-Swimming** refer to the gifts of the Spirit referenced in the book of Romans. **The eight maids a-milking** symbolize the eight Beatitudes. **The nine ladies dancing** symbolize the fruit of the Holy Spirit described in Galatians 5:22. **The ten lords a-leaping** speak of the Ten Commandments. **the eleven pipers piping** refer to the eleven faithful Apostles, and **The twelve drummers drumming** is a reference to the twelve points of belief in The Apostles' Creed.

Chapter 7

THE GOODNESS OF GOD

IT WAS THE WINTER OF 1982, AND I WAS EIGHT MONTHS PREGNANT WITH MY second child...and in grave danger. The circumstances I experienced with previous pregnancies were repeating themselves, and I developed Toxemia yet again. All the signs were there: swelling, severe headaches, dangerously elevated blood pressure, blurred vision. The troubled look on my obstetrician's face that morning in his office spoke volumes. The twinkle was gone from his eyes, and his grandfatherly face displayed deep worry. Dr. McCandry had been my doctor for two years, and had seen me through an emotionally painful miscarriage. My first baby had survived a very complicated pregnancy due to my toxemic state, but I had not been as fortunate with my second pregnancy. Now in the eighth month of my third pregnancy the situation was serious. Dr. McCandry's voice was heavy as he spoke. "Your blood pressure's way too high," he said. "I want you to check yourself into City Hospital. Today." "Is that really necessary?" I asked, a little shocked. I shouldn't have been. Dr. McCandry had been expressing concern over my rising blood pressure for months. Experiments with several medications to control my hypertension had yielded no results, and I was now out of options. "Yes," he replied. "Not only are you at risk of a stroke or epileptic seizures, but your elevated blood pressure is endangering your baby. I can't treat you here, you need to be hospitalized."

I dutifully did as I was told, and drove home to collect my things, numb from fear. I related all this to my husband. He jumped into action, brought our three-year-old to a friend's house, and drove me to the hospital. Neither of us spoke on the short ride there. The fear felt like a foreign object lodged in my throat, preventing words from escaping. When we arrived at the hospital I clutched the door handle for a moment, a helpless gesture to delay a flood of events that would soon overtake me, and carry me to unknown places I feared.

After the preliminary hospital check-in, I was taken to a room and attached to numerous graph-type machines. Each machine monitored a different function, and one displayed the baby's heartbeat. The screen showed the baby's heartbeat was erratic, a sign that my elevated blood pressure was affecting the baby's condition. The nurse assisting me was watching the screens intently over her wire-rimmed classes, which sat just above the tip of her nose. "We need to induce labor on you, Hon," she informed me. "Your doctor said we can't wait." She was a trim, energetic, middle-aged woman with short reddish hair, who had seen her share of deliveries. "I'm going to give you a shot of Pitocin to start your labor."

"Where is my doctor?" I asked.

"He's on his way," she replied. "By the time you're ready to go, he'll be here." She then administered the drug, and we waited and watched the data displayed on the various screens.

But an odd thing happened...or didn't happen. I didn't respond to the drug. The anticipated labor pains never began. I was no stranger to Pitocin, having received it with my first baby, and he was delivered safely. But nothing about this pregnancy was normal. My blood pressure continued to climb, and now the monitors revealed the baby showed signs of fetal distress.

At that moment Dr. McCandry walked into the room, already suited up in surgical scrubs. He was quiet, which was unusual for him, and I could see the look of concern on his face. "Rosalie," he said urgently, "we're going to have to deliver your baby by C-Section. We can't wait any longer." I nodded weakly, tears welling up in my eyes. A C-Section was the only option now, and time was of the essence. My husband returned from donning surgical scrubs too, and took my hand as I was wheeled into an operating room - not a delivery room. The temperature of the brightly lit room was ice cold, and lying on the metal table I shivered. Around me the surgical team was a flurry of silent activity. Before pulling his surgical mask up, Dr. McCandry gave me a reassuring smile that quickly vanished as he nodded to the Anesthesiologist to begin. Restraints were tied to my arms, and a needle that seemed a foot long was injected into my spine to numb the lower half of my body. At that point my fear escalated from gripping to crushing, and I was acutely aware that I could hyperventilate if I didn't control my fear. I fervently prayed in silence for God to deliver my baby and me through this trial alive. Medical technology in 1982 was far from where it is today. As the baby was only eight months along in development, we could expect problems.

A screen was erected to obstruct my view of the surgery. My husband continued to hold my hand comfortingly, while he intently observed the operation. Something about his intense study of the procedure gave me a small, inexplicable sense of normalcy and comfort, as though he were a student in a classroom, not observing a potential life-and-death procedure. But that small, imagined respite from fear was shattered in an instant by the look of alarm on Dr. McCandry's face. My husband shared the same look, and his body stiffened as he stared in shock and disbelief. The surgical team was equally silent as they studied Dr. McCandry's face for some reaction. Everyone remained speechless and motionless as they watched the Doctor carefully free the baby from his maternal haven, and supporting his tiny body with one hand, gently unwrap the umbilical cord from around the baby's neck with the other....three times. Even a layman, such as my husband, knew what that meant. If my body had responded to the Pitocin and the baby had been delivered naturally, he would have strangled in the birth canal. Dr. McCandry, a devout Christian, uttered "Glory to God, Glory to God," almost in disbelief.

But there was no time for rejoicing. As his lungs were not yet completely developed, my baby struggled to breathe, which was evident by the bluish color of his skin. He wasn't even able to cry. As soon as he was delivered he was whisked away to an oxygen unit. And before my surgery was completed a Paramedic appeared holding my baby in a carrier. He kindly let me stroke the baby's tiny arm for only a second. "We have to hurry," he said. "His lungs aren't fully developed and he's having trouble breathing on his own." Then the baby was swiftly transported, via ambulance, to a Children's Hospital Neonatal Unit. I later learned that while en route he stopped breathing completely, but was miraculously revived by the incredibly competent team of Paramedics.

As my blood pressure was not stabilizing, I remained hospitalized for days, unable to see or hold my baby. I was so ill it was a struggle to lift my head, my vision was blurred, and the crushing headache from the epidural was unrelenting. I wasn't being given details about the baby's condition from the Neonatal staff when I called, as there were none to give, and this only served to increase my fears. I believed my baby had died, and no one would tell me because of my precarious physical condition. I was convinced they were worried such intense grief would push me over the edge, and leave my other child without a mother. I have never cried that much before, or since. I begged my husband to tell me if our baby had died, but he repeatedly insisted that Justin - the name we had chosen for him months before, was alive and improving now, after some initial challenges. "He's getting oxygen 'round the clock," he said, "and he's not out of the woods yet. But at six pounds, he's a good size, and that will help him." I drew comfort from his words, and felt a small measure of relief from the agonizing fear that had been tormenting me for days. "Thank God," I sighed.

Finally my husband brought me a photo of Justin, with an oxygen tube taped to his little face, and all sorts of wires and monitors attached to his tiny body. But he was alive, and I stared at that beautiful picture for days, until I was at last discharged and could see and hold my precious little son myself. His survival wasn't completely real for me until that moment. The compassionate staff at Children's Hospital allowed our little family to visit Justin as often as we wished. My three-year-old, Max, was adorable in a surgical gown so long that all you could see were the tops of his sneakers. Nothing did more to lift my spirits than to see the progress Justin was making daily, and at two weeks of age he had made enough progress to come home. Despite his tentative start in life, Justin thrived and did not experience any health issues resulting from his premature birth. Today, forty-two years later, that tiny, struggling newborn is a healthy, strapping young man.

God performed a miracle in my life all those years ago. Although it hasn't been the only one, the miracle of Justin's birth remains, by far, the greatest.

A MOTHER'S BLANKET OF PRAYER

When you were young
And it was cold outside,
With a blanket
I covered you with care.

Now that you are older
And the world is much colder,
I cover you with
A blanket of prayer.

Author unknown

Chapter 8
GOD'S WORD IN
ALL SEASONS

THE KNOWLEDGE DERIVED FROM GOD'S WORD IS UNLIKE ANY OTHER TYPE OF knowledge, in that it is necessary for survival in a fallen world. As most people, I find I have better memorization of Scripture when I fully understand the verse I'm studying. God's Word abounds with many layers of meaning, so I will read the interpretations provided by my Bible, as well as pray for divine understanding. This practice is especially effective when I can relate the verse to a situation I have faced, or am currently experiencing.

As visual imagery is prevalent throughout the Bible, it's not hard to connect a descriptive verse of Scripture with a mental picture. When my eldest son was deployed to a makeshift outpost in Afghanistan, I visualized the powerful battlefield images from Psalm 91. I drew strength and comfort daily from King David's expressions of reliance upon his God to deliver him, and paralleled them to my son's dangerous combat situation. I have an emotional attachment to Psalm 91 now, and I don't think I will ever forget it because of the personal meaning it holds for me.

The more we delve into God's Word, the more our understanding of who God is will increase. A believer cannot experience true victory over the world without total surrender and obedience to the Lord. This results in a highly communicative relationship between God and believer. There is ongoing engagement with the Lord, receiving His responses directly to our spirits, and through Scripture. God will confirm a word given through divine guidance, provision, open doors, and occasionally through another believer. As any good parent, God is not silent toward His children.

At times, the Lord will reveal something significant to us when we least expect it. He has recently made me aware how imperative it is to share Jesus with as many people as possible, now more than ever. If someone doesn't know Jesus, any interaction at all, however brief, is an opportunity to witness to him/her. That includes individuals who are difficult, and those we may not be fond of. I now understand that God allows some people to try our patience to the utmost, so we don't overlook them. We won't soon forget a disagreeable individual, however brief the encounter. It's very easy to pray for people we like, but how many of us will pray for a difficult person, especially when he/she is not part of our daily lives? And it's that very individual who most likely is greatly in need of salvation, as well as healing.

Recently, I was grumbling to myself about an acquaintance with an overbearing personality. I was thinking of smart retorts to her sarcastic mode of communication, when God stopped me in my tracks with this question, "What gives you the right to decide she should go to Hell?" I was stunned, and responded, "How am I consigning her to Hell, Lord?" He then replied, "She's in your life for a reason. If you allow offense to prevent you from witnessing to her, she may never experience redemption. Do you really want to see her suffer for all eternity, because your hurt feelings mean more to you than her salvation?" Needless to say, this exchange cut me to the quick. I was ashamed and repentant for allowing my emotions to supersede the importance of sharing the message of salvation with this woman. I realized how selfish I was being, and that I have been equally selfish with others I was not fond of. This unexpected, deeply personal and revealing experience with the Lord opened my eyes, and truly changed my heart.

Sadly, a hardness of heart toward God is a condition that continues to afflict people, even those who love Jesus. Great is the desire to remain in a comfortable niche, carved through years of closing one's eyes to any idea that challenges established knowledge. Jesus often addressed the mindset that prevents believers from experiencing total victory in Him. "Do you not yet perceive or understand? Is your heart still hardened? Having eyes do you not see, and having ears do you not hear? And do you not remember?" (Mark 8:17-18) It cannot be emphasized enough that a complete and total trust in the absolute goodness of God is essential to a deep, personal walk with Him. The closer we draw to the Lord, the more we will experience His amazing, overwhelming love for us. God is not a harsh taskmaster, He doesn't want us to work for Him. Rather, He desires that we partner with Him, sharing the joys, the challenges, and the victories together. He wants us to walk in authority and power, as children of the King.

The book of Psalms reflects followers' relentless struggles to align their desires with those of God. In the Psalms, ancient Israel's reactions to events, both good and bad, are recorded. Although the emotions run the range from joy to utter despair, the Israelites were left fundamentally unchanged by the blessings and miracles of God on their behalf. The majority of God's chosen people routinely forgot His goodness as soon as the current danger had passed. What caused the nation of Israel to have such a short memory?

The Lord's prophets, on the other hand, freely expressed gratitude and praise, and their minds were stayed upon the Lord continually. In contrast to the people of Israel, the prophets shared a one-on-one relationship with God. The Lord's prophets and priests made intercession with God on behalf of the people, and this arrangement characterized ancient Israel's culture and worship. "Speak to us yourself and we will listen. But do not have God speak to us or we will die." (Exodus 20:19) As a result, the Israelites themselves experienced little spiritual growth and maturity. In the Psalms, ancient Israel's spiritual immaturity is reflected; crying out to God amidst troubles that resulted from their faithlessness, and calling upon the Lord to curse those who threatened them. When people have a "go-between" God and themselves, the need for intimacy with God is diminished. They are usually content with repetitive rituals, and all the worship and communication with God is assumed by the intercessor. In ancient Israel's case these tasks fell to the priests and the prophets.

The ancient Hebrews viewed God, and life, in black-and-white terms. They reasoned that good things should happen to good people, while terrible curses should befall the perpetrators of evil. So often when Israel was beset with troubles, the Psalmist chronicled the people's questioning of God and turning away in discouragement, revealing a common misplacement of faith as a key issue in Israel's worship. As 1 Samuel 4:3-11 demonstrates, the Israelites favored rituals and artifacts to personal fellowship with God. After experiencing defeat in battle with the Philistines, rather than fall on their faces before the Lord, Israel chose instead to have the Ark of the Covenant transported to them from Shiloh. They reasoned the Ark would protect them from their battle-seasoned enemies. But even the holy Ark of God's Covenant with Isael was no substitute for personally entering the Lord's presence through praise and worship, and ask Him for deliverance. If Israel had turned to God, and allowed Him to soften their hearts toward Him, He likely would have given them victory over the Philistines, sparing 30,000 needless Hebrew deaths. It's clear that had His people remained faithful to Him, God in turn would have made Israel undefeatable and wildly favored, for His glory. But despite God's passionate love for Israel, and glorious manifestations of power, the Israelites continued to reject Him, and turn repeatedly to objects, and false, inanimate gods. Sadly, most of humanity has continued down the same path for millennia, placing faith in things and people above the Lord.

Struggles and temptations designed to hinder us from God's plan for our lives are relentless. But the Lord's goodness and might are far more powerful than any obstacle we will ever encounter in this life. Intimate fellowship with God, combined with knowledge of His Holy, inerrant Word, empower us to successfully navigate the treacherous highways and byways of this fallen world, and bring the light of Jesus to those in darkness. "Incline your ear and hear the words of the wise, And apply your heart to My knowledge..." (Prov. 22:17)

Blessed journey, fellow Traveler.

THE END

ABOUT THE AUTHOR

Rosalie is a surrendered servant of the Lord Jesus Christ, and the Author of Letter to an Unbeliever, and A Summer In The Desert. Rosalie makes her home in San Diego, California, and is the mother of four grown sons.

Printed in the United States
by Baker & Taylor Publisher Services